Copyright 2023 © Donna Tadych
Mommy, Mommy How Does My Heart Work?

Written by: Donna Tadych
Illustrations by: Phillip Ortiz & Rebekah Gangruth
Designed by Peel Creative, peel-creative.com

All scripture references from:
New American Standard Bible
The Passion Translation Bible
Psalm 139 is a modified version of the New American Standard Version.

Published by: Donna Tadych

ISBN: 979-8-9882060-0-2

Table of Contents

Dedication

This book was dropped into my heart a long time ago and it has been carried inside my heart through my healing journey. It is a joy to see it come forth into the hands of children and adults so they can know how awesomely and wonderfully they are made. This is for each of you.

To the many who have sat with me and loved me back to life (You know who you are!). I am eternally grateful to each one of you! Thank you! This book is living proof of the outcome of loving well with His love.

I also dedicate this book to my children, my grandchildren and the many generations to come. May each of you live wholeheartedly and be who He designed you to be and out of being YOU have influence and impact in partnership with Him that lasts for eternity.

FORWARD

It is with great joy that I take pen in hand to write a forward for Donna's book—a book that takes the principles of **HeartSync Ministry** and makes them applicable for working with children and families.

The **HeartSync Ministry** vision is to promote and participate in the primary mission statement of Christ to *"heal the brokenhearted" (Luke 4:17-18a)*, whereby He gives us (undivided hearts) a singleness of heart and action *(Jer. 32:39)* to the end that we are more fully able to *"love the Lord our God with all our heart and with all our soul and with all our mind" (Mat. 22:37)*. **HeartSync Ministry** does this by intentionally synchronizing, or connecting with the various aspects of the heart and bringing them into full relationship with God.

It has been well over thirty-five years since I was called into this mission of working with the brokenhearted. In the early years, as I encountered the severely brokenhearted—one person after another—I was trying to gain some kind of understanding both as a clinician and a minister, about the variables involved in how the human heart breaks or becomes divided. What became obvious was that there were four major areas of the heart with definitive roles, and that each of these areas could present with varying degrees of brokenness depending on the level of trauma that these persons had experienced at critical junctures in development. In 2005, I began a research project to consider whether or not these areas—what I now refer to as core heart parts—were apparent in all people. After a year of research and seventeen subsequent years of doing **HeartSync Ministry**, I remain thoroughly convinced that absolutely all people present with at least these four core parts, or their roles. The four core heart parts are as follows:

1. The True Self—that is the true heart or essence of the self, and which has the capacity to connect most strongly with God.

2. The Function Core—that does the daily functioning of life and left brain logical reasoning, but keeps a distance from emotional pain that inhibits the ability to function.

3. The Emotion Core—that does both positive and negative emotion, but for the purposes of healing, is most closely connected to and holds unresolved negative emotion, pain and trauma.

4. The Guardian Core—that does the classic fight or flight responses, and believes that emotional pain and trauma must be kept away from the Function aspect of the heart, or the Function aspect will be too overwhelmed and unable to do daily functioning.

Two additional and astounding findings from my research indicated that for the average Christian believer it is rare for more than two of the core parts to be in relationship with God, and that the Guardian aspect of the heart is almost never in relationship with God. I believe these findings to be incredibly significant in the world of healing prayer, since we can now, armed with this knowledge, intentionally engage these aspects of the heart and work to resolve the conflicts and spiritual oppression that are keeping them separated from God.

Donna Tadych has been working for some time, to make these findings useful in her work with families and children. In the fall of 2022, it was my great joy to join her in teaching the first "*HeartSync for Kids*" course. I am excited to endorse the importance of this project—making the **HeartSync** principles understandable to children and their parents. Armed with this information, we have found that children can easily be led to navigate their internal conflicts that often result in painful behavior—providing them with the necessary vocabulary to talk about what is happening in their hearts, and then resolve it by interacting with the Lord. This often results in the child's ability to more fully walk in what Jesus called the *"sum of the law and the prophets,"* to love the Lord their God with all their heart, soul, and mind.

What a joy it is to consider that the use of the truths contained in this book will assist children in resolving issues of their hearts, so that they will have the necessary skills and accompanying spiritual development to use through the entirety of their lives—unlike many of us adults that were well into adulthood before we could find the tools needed to enhance this love relationship. For these reasons and more, I heartily bless Donna in bringing forth this important work.

The Rev. Andrew Miller, LCSW
Executive Director of HeartSync Ministries

Mommy, Mommy... How Does My Heart Work Book Guide:

Dear Reader,

Whether you are reading this book to children in your life or gleaning for yourself, it will open your heart and eyes to see part of God's blueprint and design of the heart. We each have a physical heart that beats and pumps blood so we can live and move and be alive. Our Inside Heart is also part of what makes us alive. In Him, we live and move and have our being whether we acknowledge God or not. God loves us either way but He really desires to have relationship with us so we can:

- **Discover our True Self and BE who we are designed by God to BE**
- **Function by figuring things out with God and not live confused**
- **Guard with an upgraded way of protecting the heart with Him and be God defended**
- **Emotion experiences love and has God's help to carry pain instead of hurting alone**

You can use the book by:

1. As shared above, read and see how the heart is made.

2. Establish this concrete language with children so that they can explain what is happening in their own heart and identify the heart talk i.e. self talk that is happening inside of them too.

3. Have heart conversations with children and use the book as a concrete, visual illustration.

4. When they are struggling with a specific area of the heart or they are in a tug-of-war between parts of their heart, then you can turn to those areas of the heart and read about them again.

5. When you want to talk about True Self and go on the discovery of who they are made to BE then you can use this section of the book to show the abstract in a concrete way.

6. If you are struggling yourself no matter what your age is, read this with a childlike heart and eyes so you can know your own heart design and connect with the one who designed you too.

7. If you have experienced difficulty, pain and trauma that caused your own or children's hearts you know have heart break, go on the heart journey with God because He binds up the broken hearted and sets us free to live wholeheartedly.

8. If you want to learn how all the heart can fit and work together the way God designed, then keep reading this book over and over so that your heart can do the same.

It is my deep desire for this to be a resource that you can use to grow in understanding and connection with God, within yourself and with others. May we each enter into wholehearted living with God as we live out our Unique God Design identity and destiny.

Many Blessings,

Donna Tadych

Mommy, Mommy
HOW DOES MY HEART WORK?

Donna Tadych
with Father Andrew Miller, LCSW

Illustrations by: Phillip Ortiz & Rebekah Gangruth

Mommy, Mommy...... How does my heart work?

That is a great question.
I love your questions and I am so glad God has answers for us both.

Well, let's start at the beginning of you. Who made you to be you?

Psalm 139:13-17 says
"For God created my innermost parts;
You weaved me together in my Mom's womb
I will give thanks to You because
I am awesomely and wonderfully made;
Wonderful are Your works God,
And my heart knows it very well.
My frame was not hidden from You God
When I was made in secret,
And skillfully formed in the depths of the earth.
God, Your eyes have seen my formless substance
And in Your book were written all the days of my life
When there was not one of them yet.
How precious also are Your thoughts for me God!
How vast is the sum of them."

So God created me and put my inside parts together? God even designed my heart? Yes, He made your heart. He put you together in a unique and special way to be you!

He made the physical heart in your body that beats so you can play and have fun and do all you were created to do.

Can you feel your physical heartbeat?

God also made your inside heart in a similar way.
They both have four parts like a puzzle that makes one heart.

*Do you
like puzzles?*

Let's look at the four pieces
of your heart puzzle.

Let's ask God to help us
understand how He made
each part.

THE FUNCTION
HEART PART

MY THINK, TALK,
KNOW, TO DO,
TIME PART

God designed the Function Heart Part to help you think, talk and do the "to do's" of your day.

When you eat.....

When you make your bed......

When you get dressed.....

When you play games......

When you do your school work and learn.......

When you are keeping track of
time and all you have to do......

Your Function Heart Part is helping you to do all of those things and more. It helps keep track of things that are important priorities and reminds you what you need to do.

Wow! I really need this part. It helps me do so much.

Yes, God knew what He was doing when He designed you. That is part of what makes you wonderfully made by Him.

THE EMOTION HEART PART

MY INSIDE CUPS THAT HOLD ALL OF MY FEELINGS PART

God designed the Emotion Heart Part to help hold all of your feelings. It is like a cup that fills up or is empty. It can get as big as it needs to to hold all you feel.

Have you ever seen a pond, a lake or the ocean?

Your Emotion Heart Part can hold your feelings like these hold water.

It can be filled with happy and joyful feelings.
It can also be filled with sad or mad feelings.

You can even have more than one feeling at the same time and different Emotion Heart Part cups fill up. This can make it feel like your cups are heavy and full of "Feeling" rocks. When some cups are empty, then other cups get full.

What are some feelings
you have that fill up
your Emotion Heart
Part cups?

What happens to you that makes you feel:

Joyful or Happy?

Excited!?

Loved or Wanted?

Calm or Peaceful?

Grateful, Thankful?

Thank you

Silly and Funny!?

What happens to you that makes you feel:

Sad, Overwhelmed?

Mad or Angry?

Scared or Afraid?

Worried,
Anxious?

Embarrassed,
or Shame?

Rejected,
Not Wanted
or Included?

God designed your Emotion Heart Part to hold all of these feelings and many more.

Did you know that even God has emotions? He created you to be like Him.

Emotion Heart Part helps you experience life more fully.

Think of Emotions or feelings as colors that help your life pictures be bright.

Can you see the difference without colors?

All emotions and feelings are ok because God made them. What you do with the feelings when your cups get full makes a difference.

Wow! The Emotion Heart Part is important too.

Yes, this part helps you experience connection with Him and with others. This part helps you feel His love and mine too!

He enjoys you so much and so do I!

THE GUARD HEART PART

MY PROTECTOR OF MY HEART PART

Did you know that your heart is like a kingdom
and it needs to be protected?

God says in Proverbs 4:23:

" Watch over your heart with all diligence. "

That means to guard carefully what you let
through the gate of your heart.

The third part of your heart that God designed when He
made you is your Guard Heart Part.

This part is like a gatekeeper that watches over your heart
to decide what is good, bad or scary. It decides what to let
into your heart kingdom.

It also decides what to do if bad or scary things break into
your heart kingdom even if you didn't want to let them in.

The Guard Heart Part is like a knight that protects the kingdom of your heart. Guard serves God who is the King of all kings.

The Guard Heart Part is also like a sheep dog that protects the sheep - the other parts of your heart - from wolves and harmful things that try to hurt your heart parts.

We are sometimes called God's sheep.

"We are His people and the sheep of His pasture."

Psalm 100:3 NASB

The Sheepdog serves the Shepherd.

Jesus is even called the Good Shepherd because He takes good care of us.

Sheep can't defend themselves and that's why they need the Shepherd and Sheepdog or Guard Heart Part.

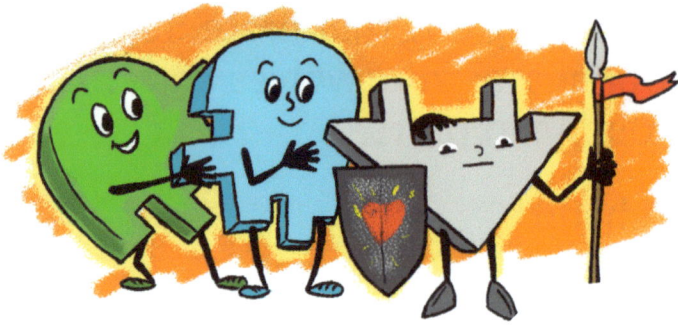

God designed the Guard Part of the heart to protect your other heart parts. He commands Guard Part to do this so it will always have this job.

God wants to teach Guard Part His way of how to guard carefully with diligence and also give Guard Part the strength and courage to do it because God will do it with Guard Heart Part.

Wow! I must be very valuable for God to make Guard Part to guard over the kingdom of my heart

Yes, you are His treasure. You are His child and His love demonstrated by Jesus reveals your value. You are so valuable to Him and to me!

THE TRUE SELF
HEART PART

THE REAL ME PART,

WHO HE DESIGNED
ME TO BE PART

Did you know that you have a special, unique God print on your thumbprint?

Let's look at it now. No one else has the same print as you.

Just like God made your thumbprint unique and special, He made your heart print that way too.

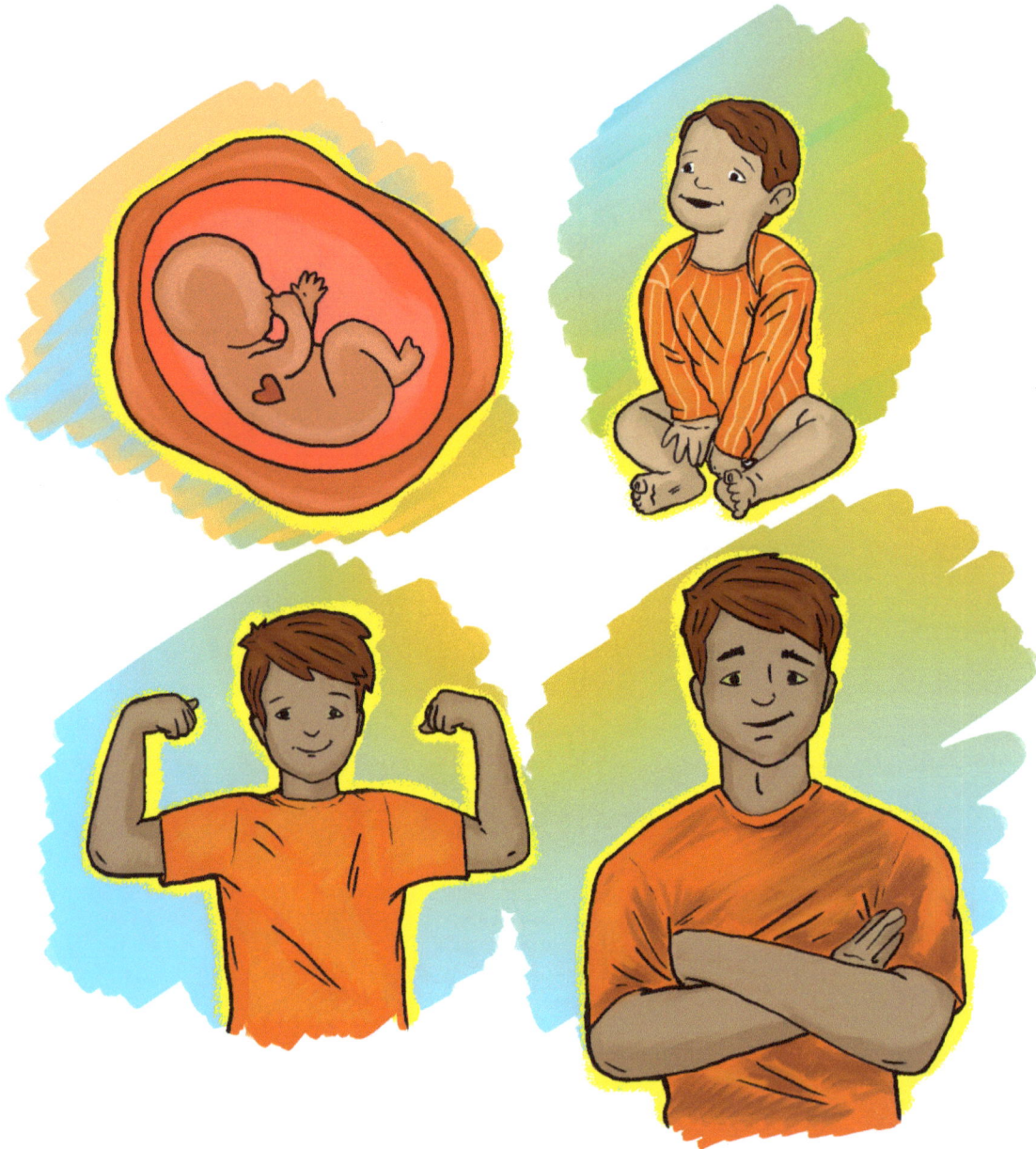

There is only 1 of YOU!
This is your True Self Heart Part.
This is who God designed you to BE.
This is the fourth part to your heart puzzle.
It is who you really are and all you will become as you grow up.

Did you know that inside every acorn is everything needed to become an entire oak tree?

Your True Self Heart Part is just like that.

When you plant an acorn, it has the potential to grow...so do YOU!

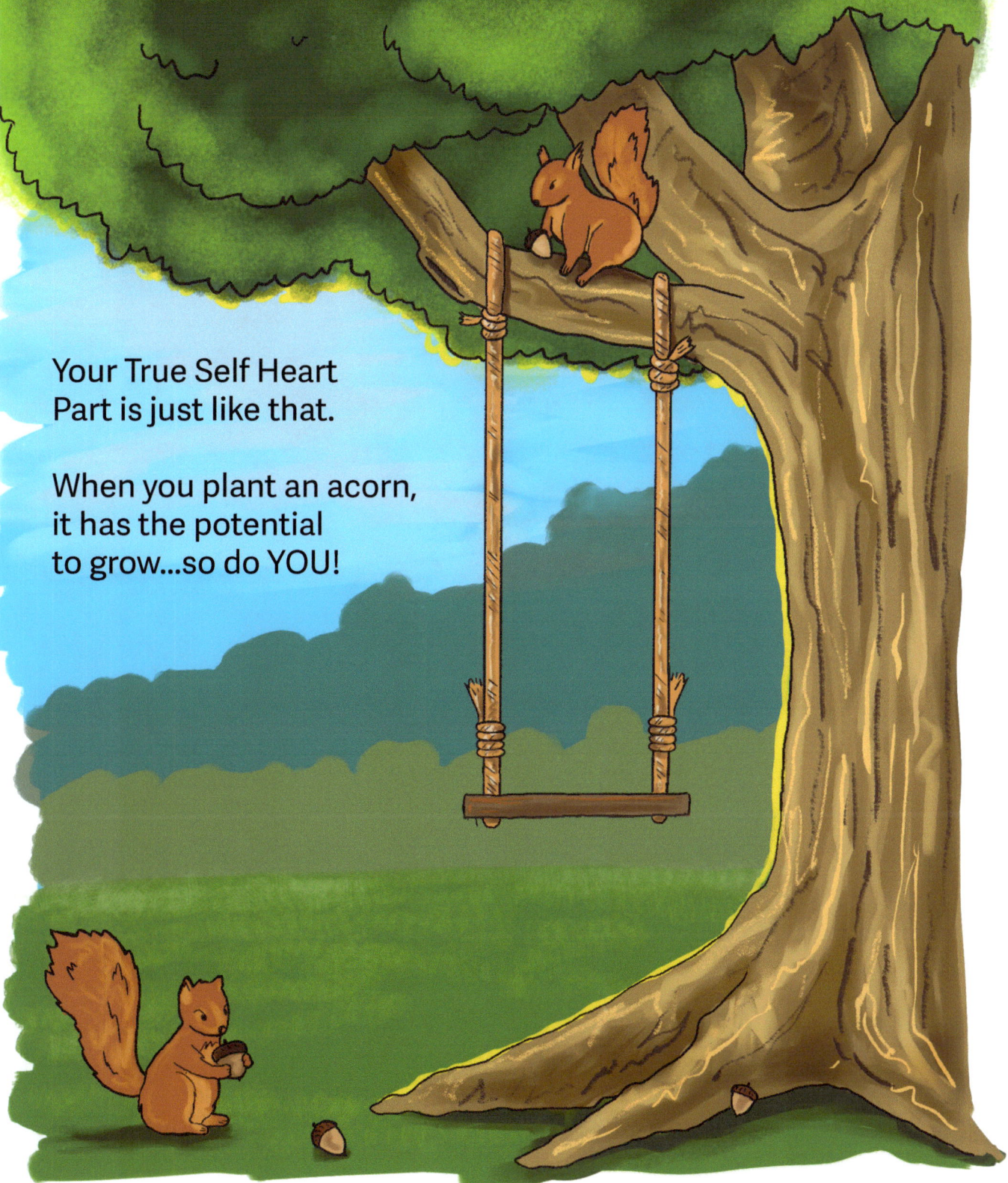

When your True Self Heart Part connects with God, it unlocks the potential to grow up and become all He designed you to BE.

Your True Self Heart Part is also like a locked treasure chest or gift box waiting to be opened with His unique key for your heart.

Unlocked, your True Self ...... the real you....
you were created to BE gets discovered.

You find YOU inside your heart and with
God you become your TRUE Self!

Remember........

Don't stop until you
finish your journey
Of Becoming YOU!

Every part of your heart puzzle is important and designed by God. Remember Psalm 139 says ...

"You are awesomely and wonderfully made!"

He created you to connect with Him and for all your heart parts to fit and work together just like a puzzle so you can experience His love fully and love Him and others wholeheartedly.

Wow! I really am awesomely and wonderfully made by God. He designed me and I am the only one like me.

Yes, you are an original masterpiece.

God's thoughts of you really do outnumber the sands of the sea and every one of them is filled with love for YOU!

ADDITIONAL RESOURCES

For more information about Donna Tadych and Wisdom's Way:

The Family Wisdom's Way podcast
https://familywisdomsway.libsyn.com/

The Wisdom's Way website
https://findwisdomsway.com/

Contact information:
findwisdomsway@gmail.com

About Father Andrew Miller, LCSW and HeartSync Ministries:

Father Andrew Miller, LCSW is the Founder and President of HeartSync Ministries. He has practiced as a professional individual, marriage and family therapist since 1990. The bulk of his practice is focused on resolving severe desynchronization (scriptural brokenheartedness) in those suffering from abuse and trauma. He actively incorporates biblical healing principles with sound clinical practice.

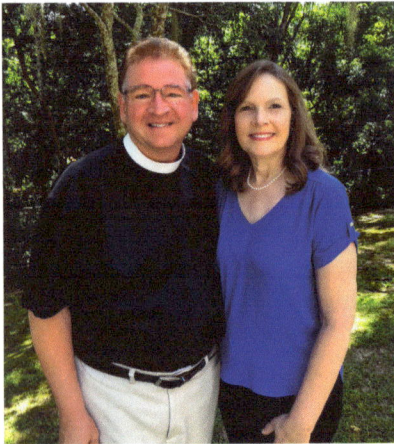

Andrew holds two undergraduate degrees from Florida State University's College of Arts and Sciences in Biological Sciences with a minor in Chemistry, as well as a degree in Math and Science Education. He acquired his Master's Degree in Clinical Social Work from the School of Social Work at Florida State University.

In 2009, Andrew was ordained as a priest in the Orthodox Evangelical Episcopal Church. He and his wife Lisa subsequently founded HeartSync Ministries in 2010. In recognition of that calling, he was made a Canon Missioner of Healing in 2013. He served as the Founding Director of Tallahassee Healing Prayer Ministries for ten years–a position that he left in 2016 to focus more fully on HeartSync Ministries. Andrew serves as Chaplain to the Archbishop, Dr. Russell McClanahan.

Since the launching of HeartSync Ministries, he now travels nationally and internationally several times a year to do seminars, presenting a vision for how to use the HeartSync modality in prayer ministry. Andrew currently resides in Tallahassee with his wife, Lisa.

The HeartSync Ministries website
https://heartsyncministries.org